Take a trip down memory lane with this look back at 1952. "I Love Lucy" is the top show on TV; Ike wins the presidency in a landslide; the Korean War enters its 3rd year; singer Eddie Fisher has his first #1 hit; Marilyn Monroe is the hottest rising young star; and the New York Yankees win their 4th straight World Series. Remember the stories, pictures, people and events that made 1952 your special year!

A walk back in time...

To:

From:

Managing Editor • Art Worthington

Publishers • Lawrence Siegel & Art Worthington

Design • Peter Hess & Marguerite Jones

Writing & Research • Laurie Cohn & Peter Hess

Facilitator • Pamela Thomas

(800) 541-3533

GENE KELLY
DONALD O'CONNOR
DEBBIE REYNOLDS
Singin'
In The Rain

JOHN WAYNE
MAUREEN O'HARA
The Quiet Man

GARY COOPER
High Noon

what's
playing
at the

MOVIES

Monkey Business • Moulin R
Rachel

AHOY! A HOWL!
They're Raising Cain
on the Bounding Main!

WARNER BROS. SUPER CINE COLOR

ABBOTT and COSTELLO
MEET CAPTAIN K
CHARLES
LAUGHTON

ALDO RAY

M·G·M PRESENTS
SPENCER
TRACY
KATHARINE
HEPBURN

Together again—
and it's
no fib.
Their
funniest
hit since
"Adam's Rib"

PAT
AND
MIKE

WILLIAM CHING
GEORGE CUKOR LAWRENCE WEINGARTEN

Cecil B. DeMille's
THE
GREATEST
SHOW
ON
EARTH
Color by Technicolor

JAMES STEWART

Singin' In T
Snows Of
Me • Som
hing To Live
Of Paleface

MGM
LANA
TURNER
KIRK
DOUGLAS
WALTER
PIDGEON
DICK
POWELL

The
Bad
And
The
Beautiful

BARRY
SULLIVAN
GLORIA
GRAHAME
GILBERT
ROLAND

GRAHAME

Cineran
ashingto
harley • with A Song In

TOP BOX OFFICE STARS OF
1952

Gary Cooper
Bing Crosby
Doris Day
Susan Hayward
Bob Hope
Jerry Lewis
& Dean Martin
Gregory Peck
Randolph Scott
James Stewart
John Wayne

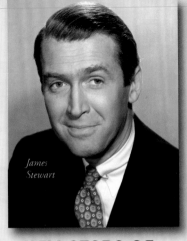

James Stewart

NEW STARS OF
1952

Marge & Gower
Champion
Mitzi Gaynor
Rock Hudson
Kim Hunter
Marilyn Monroe
Audie Murphy
Debbie Reynolds
Danny Thomas
Forrest Tucker
David Wayne

Marilyn Monroe

FilmClips

Humphrey Bogart relaxes with his Oscar® after receiving the Best Actor award for his performance in 1951's THE AFRICAN QUEEN.

The first Cinerama feature, THIS IS CINERAMA, thrills audiences with panoramic color image and stereo sound.

Gloria Grahame wins the Best Supporting Actress Oscar® for her role in 1952's THE BAD AND THE BEAUTIFUL, a melodrama about career climbing in Hollywood.

Gloria Grahame

The National Board of Review of Motion Pictures votes SINGIN' IN THE RAIN one of the best pictures of 1952.

Gene Kelly

Filming on ROMAN HOLIDAY starring Gregory Peck and Audrey Hepburn is scheduled to begin in Rome. The story is said to be based on Princess Margaret's romps in Italy.

Oscars® Presented in 1952
for 1951 films

BEST PICTURE
An American In Paris

BEST ACTOR
Humphrey Bogart, *The African Queen*

BEST ACTRESS
Vivien Leigh, *A Streetcar Named Desire*

BEST DIRECTOR
George Stevens, *A Place In The Sun*

BEST SUPPORTING ACTOR
Karl Malden, *A Streetcar Named Desire*

BEST SUPPORTING ACTRESS
Kim Hunter, *A Streetcar Named Desire*

Oscars® Presented in 1953
for 1952 films

BEST PICTURE
The Greatest Show On Earth

BEST ACTOR
Gary Cooper, *High Noon*

BEST ACTRESS
Shirley Booth, *Come Back, Little Sheba*

BEST DIRECTOR
John Ford, *The Quiet Man*

BEST SUPPORTING ACTOR
Anthony Quinn, *Viva Zapata!*

BEST SUPPORTING ACTRESS
Gloria Grahame, *The Bad And The Beautiful*

1952 Advertisement

"Let's go, Mr. Dreamer, that television set won't help you shovel the walk."

SIMPLIFIED, SINGLE-CONTROL TUNING. Remarkable Target Tuner perfectly synchronizes picture and sound. Filtered. Clear pictures edge to edge with no fade, no drift, no further adjustments.

NEW! ACOUSTINATOR TONE CONTROL —provides fully variable tone range, from treble to bass, for the famous "Golden Voice" sound—assures you of perfect listening enjoyment.

NO GLARE ANNOYANCE. Exclusive Glare Guard eliminates up to 90% of reflected glare. Optically curved screen and non reflecting Absorbalite tube direct outside light interference down and away from the screen, out of eye range ... for greater viewing comfort.

© 1952, MOTOROLA INC. *Specifications subject to change without notice*

ELEVISION DEBUTS

dventures
f Superman

he Adventures of
Ozzie & Harriet

andstand

eath Valley Days

he Ernie Kovacs Show

he Guiding Light

Married Joan

ve Got A Secret

he Jackie Gleason Show

ur Miss Brooks

he Today Show

his Is
our Life

ictory at Sea

he Walter
Vinchell Show

Lucille Ball

TOP SHOWS ON THE TUBE

Arthur Godfrey And
His Friends

Arthur Godfrey's
Talent Scouts

The Buick Circus Hour

The Colgate
Comedy Hour

Dragnet

Fireside Theatre

Gangbusters

I Love Lucy

The Red Buttons
Show

Texaco Star Theater

You Bet Your Life

REXALL

1¢ SALE

SALE DAYS

Wednesday - Oct. 15
Thursday - - Oct. 16
Friday - - - - Oct. 17
Saturday - - - Oct. 18

Laugh with Amos 'n' Andy,
Sunday, 7:30 P.M. EST, on
CBS Radio Network for Rexall

THE **EMMY** AWARDS

SERIES

COMEDY	*I Love Lucy*
DRAMA	*Robert Montgomery Presents*
VARIETY	*Your Show Of Shows*

PERFORMERS

ACTOR	**Thomas Mitchell** *The Ford Television Theatre*
ACTRESSS	**Helen Hayes**
COMEDIAN	**Jimmy Durante**

Jimmy Durante

Helen Hayes

The first political ad appear on US TV airwaves – Adlai Stevenson buys 18 30-minute slots while Eisenhower buys more modest 20 second spo

•

American Bandstand begins as a local Philadelphia music show

•

The FCC authorizes the nation's first educational television station.

•

Joe DiMaggio Dugout, a weekly baseball series, makes its TV debut

Radio

MOST POPULAR DAYTIME PROGRAMS

Romance Of Helen Trent
Our Gal Sunday
Ma Perkins
Backstage Wife
Pepper Young's Family
Road Of Life
The Guiding Light
Aunt Jenny

The Guiding Light's
*Herb Nelson, Jone Allison
and Susan Douglas*

MOST POPULAR EVENING PROGRAMS

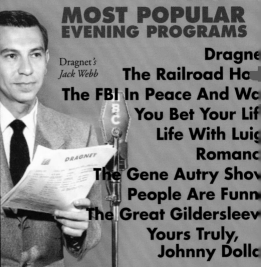

Dragnet's
Jack Webb

Dragne
The Railroad Ha
The FBI In Peace And Wo
You Bet Your Lif
Life With Luig
Romanc
The Gene Autry Show
People Are Funn
The Great Gildersleev
Yours Truly,
Johnny Dolla

TOP HITS *in* 1952
Popular Music

- *Wheel Of Fortune* — Kay Starr
- *Auf Wiederseh'n Sweetheart* — Vera Lynn
- *I Went To Your Wedding* — Patti Page
- *You Belong To Me* — Jo Stafford
- *I Saw Mommy Kissing Santa Claus* — Jimmy Boyd
- *Here In My Heart* — Al Martino
- *High Noon* — Frankie Laine
- *Blue Tango* — Leroy Anderson

Jo Stafford

Al Martino

Jimmy Boyd

Vera Lynn

1952 Advertisement

Gibson Les Paul model

It's a Sensation!

Designed by Les Paul—produced by Gibson—and enthusiastically approved by top guitarists everywhere. The Les Paul Model is a unique and exciting innovation in the fretted instrument field; you have to see and hear it to appreciate the wonderful features and unusual tone of this newest Gibson guitar. Write Dept. 101 for more information about it.

Eartha Kitt makes her nightclub singing debut with a 20-week run at New York's Blue Angel and she is featured in *New Faces of 1952* on Broadway.

Singer Eddie Fisher scores his first #1 hit with "Wish You Were Here."

Kay Starr's "Wheel of Fortune" stays at #1 for 9 weeks and she has a number of other hits on the charts as well.

Folkways Records releases the *Anthology of American Folk Music*, an influential six-album compilation comprising 84 American folk, blues and country music recordings that were originally issued from 1927 to 1932.

Blues artist Mississippi John Hurt

SMITHSONIAN FOLKWAYS RECORDINGS

ANTHOLOGY OF
AMERICAN FOLK MUSIC

EDITED BY HARRY SMITH

Rock *the Joint!*

BILL HALEY AND HIS **COMETS**

West Coast pianist/composer **Dave Brubeck** impresses the New York jazz scene with his fresh new style.

Bill Haley's "Rock the Joint!" is a milestone early rockabilly recording.

Dave Brubeck

Classical Music

At La Scala, 30-year-old **Maria Callas** receives *bravas* for her performance in Mozart's *Abduction from the Seraglio.*

Maria Callas

George and Ira Gershwin's opera *Porgy and Bess,* starring **Leontyne Price, Cab Calloway** and **William Warfield,** is sent to Europe under State Department auspices and receives ovations in Vienna and Berlin.

William Warfield, Cab Calloway and Leontyne Price in Porgy *and* Bess

Leontyne Price as Bess

Richard Tucker

LEONARD BERNSTEIN conducts his first one-act opera, *Trouble in Tahiti,* at Brandeis University.

•

Conductor **ARTURO TOSCANINI'S** hospital benefit sets advance box office sales record of $64,000.

•

Patrons in 27 cities see tenor **RICHARD TUCKER** starring in *Carmen,* the first live performance of an opera beamed via closed-circuit television directly from the Metropolitan Opera.

"CASTING LESSON IN THE BACKYARD," by Douglas Crockwell. Number 68 in the series "Home Life in America."

In this friendly, freedom-loving land
of ours—*beer belongs ... enjoy it!*

Beer and air—real-time favo

AMERICA'S BEVERAGE OF MODERATION
Sponsored by the United States Brewers Foundation...Chartered 1862

on BROADWAY

Audrey Hepburn *(left)* and Cathleen Nesbitt

Gigi
Drama adapted from the 1945 Colette novel by Anita Loos

Bette Grayson *(left)* and John Garfield

Golden Boy
Drama by Clifford Odets

1952 TONY AWARDS

PLAY
The Fourposter
Jan de Hartog (playwright)

MUSICAL
The King And I
Oscar Hammerstein II
(book/lyrics),
Richard Rodgers (music)

DRAMATIC ACTOR
José Ferrer
The Shrike

DRAMATIC ACTRESS
Julie Harris
I Am A Camera

DIRECTOR
José Ferrer
The Shrike

MUSICAL ACTOR
Phil Silvers
Top Banana

MUSICAL ACTRESS
Gertrude Lawrence
The King And I

- Special Award -
Judy Garland
for her Palace Theater performance

in the ART *world*

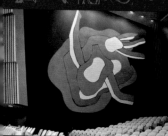

A PAIR OF **FERNAND LÉGER** MURALS ADORN THE AUDITORIUM OF THE NEW UNITED NATIONS BUILDING IN NEW YORK.

UNIVERSITY OF OHIO PROFESSOR **ROY LICHTENSTEIN** HAS A NEW YORK SHOW.

A **JACKSON POLLOCK** SHOW IN NEW YORK FEATURES **14** NEW PAINTINGS.

Jackson Pollock, Blue Poles *(detail)*, 1952

A little pain
stored in an atti
Scotland turns
to be Pieter Bruege
Christ and the Wor
Take.
Adultery fr
1565 and s
for $31,0
at a Lon
aucti

Rondanini Pie
the o
Michelang
to remain
private ha
is sol
the cit
Milan
$216,0

All America Thrills

to the Flashing

New '53 Dodge

JAM-PACKED
WITH
NEW ACTION
FEATURES

NEW 140 h.p.
Red Ram V-Eight Engine

NEW Gyro-Torque Drive
with Scat Gear

NEW Jet
Air-Flow Hood

NEW Pilot-View
Curved Windshield

NEW Travel-Lounge
Interiors

In city after city, town after town, record-breaking crowds are thronging Dodge dealer showrooms. Their enthusiastic response acclaims the '53 Dodge as the newest, nimblest piece of live action on four wheels.

New Surging Power— Beneath its low and rakish hood throbs the surging power of the mighty 140-h.p. Red Ram V-Eight . . . the most efficient engine design in any American car.

New Curve-Holding Ride—New "Stabilizer" suspension cuts side-sway, tames curves. Brings you safer, more secure "road action" in both the Coronet V-Eight Series and Meadowbrook "Six" Series.

New Sleek, Trim Action Styling— New design is low, lithe and lovely . . . yet gives more hip-room, head-room and elbow-room than ever. New Cargo-Carrier rear deck provides up to 14 cubic feet more space.

The Action Car For Active Americans

Specifications and Equipment subject to change without notice.

1952 **Notable Books**

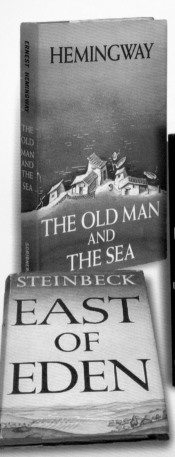

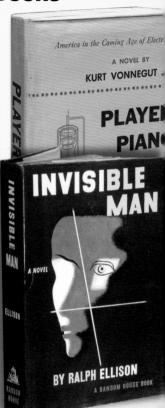

Chicago: The Second City
A.J. Liebling

The Complete Poems and Play
T.S. Eliot

The Devils of Loudun
Aldous Huxley

American Capitalism
John Kenneth Galbraith

he Far
Country
Nevil Shute

he Judgment
of Paris
Gore Vidal

iss Me, Deadly
Mickey Spillane

et It Come Down
Paul Bowles

ieutenant Hornblower
C.S. Forester

y Cousin Rachel
Daphne du Maurier

The Natural
Bernard Malamud

The Power of Positive Thinking
Norman Vincent Peale

The Rolling Stones
Robert A. Heinlein

The Thurber Album
James Thurber

Three Fine Futures for **YOU !**

PHYSICAL THERAPY

OCCUPATIONAL THERAPY

DIETITIAN

AS AN OFFICER IN THE
Women's Medical Specialist Corps
U. S. ARMY

U.S.

The *Korean* War

The third year of the effort by United Nations forces to repulse Chinese and Soviet-backed communist aggression on South Korea continues the bloody stalemate. Large-scale Allied bombing of North Korea intensifies even as armistice negotiations proceed at Kaesong.

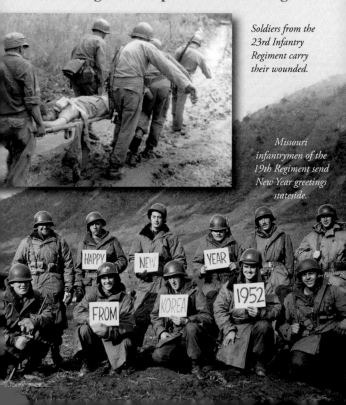

Soldiers from the 23rd Infantry Regiment carry their wounded.

Missouri infantrymen of the 19th Regiment send New Year greetings stateside.

HAPPY NEW YEAR
FROM KOREA 1952

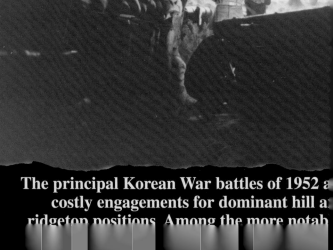

The **Korean War**

Field artillery gives support to U.S. infantrymen near Hungdung-ni.

The principal Korean War battles of 1952 a
costly engagements for dominant hill a
ridgetop positions. Among the more notab

e Battle of Old Baldy (June 26 – August 4)
e Battle of White Horse (Oct. 6 –15)
e Battle of Triangle Hill (Oct. 14 – Nov. 25)
e Battle of Hill Eerie (March 21 – June 21)

Talented enlisted men draw laughs from the front:

"Hey, fellows. Look what Special Services gave us!"

"Sure ain't hard to spot the music lovers."

"Hey, Sarge. It must be spring. Your sakura's bloomin'!"

EYE AMERICA'S
NO.1 STYLING STAR

MERCURY

TRY THE SWEEPSTA
ECONOMY CHAMPIO

YOU'RE YEARS AHEAD with Forerunner Styling! From Jet-swoop
hood to graceful rear deck—
daring, sweeping lines prove
it's new through and through.
And remember: Mercury's years-
ahead design puts you real money's ahead at trade-in time—if you
can ever bear to part with it!

Looking for style + economy
_We've got news for you

You want the smartest, most advanced car on the road, right? But
you also want economy. Can you get both in the same car? The answer,
we think, is in the year's *two* big automotive news stories. First . . .

MERCURY LEADS THE INDUSTRY WITH FORERUNNER STYLING

Your own eyes will give you the good news. You'll see at once that
Mercury is new in a fresh and daring way that makes other "new"
cars look old. You'll also see that Mercury is loaded with exciting
new Future Features . . . like the Interceptor instrument panel . . .
Space-planned interior. But here's the best news of all:

MERCURY AGAIN WINS MOBILGAS ECONOMY RUN

Yes, this massive Mercury—with the stepped-up V-8—is pound for
pound the most economical car in America today. Mercury, with
optional overdrive, has taken top honors in its class in the Mobilgas
Economy Run for three straight years—twice won the ton-mile Grand
Sweepstakes. Drop in at your Mercury dealer's today and prove it all
for yourself. You've got nothing to lose . . . except any old ideas you
may have about big, beautiful cars being expensive!

MERCURY DIVISION   •   FORD MOTOR COMPANY

BERLIN A TALE OF TWO CITIES

onditions can be really rugged in the city of Berlin, hose split personality is controlled in the East by the ussians and in the West by the Allied Command. West erlin police check incoming vehicles for contraband. uch measures are necessary to protect the Western one's economy and its German mark currency.

1. It looks like the crew bagged a smuggler.

2. Here's the contraband—parts of furniture in this false compartment.

3. More discoveries are made in the double roof including stockings and bales of textiles.

4. The smuggled goods are confiscated and added to a mounting collection in the warehouse.

3 Queens in Mourning

Queen Elizabeth II; her grandmother, Que[en] Mary; and her mother, Queen Elizabeth, t[he] Queen Mother, at the February 16th funer[al] of King George VI. Elizabeth II became Qu[een] of England upon the death of her father.

The
United Nations
General
Assembly
convenes for
the first time
in its new
$68 million
permanent
headquarters
in New York.

West Germany
signs a treaty
with Israel
committing to
pay $822
million to
indemnify
Jews for Nazi
anti-Semitic
acts during
World War II.

Coup in Cuba

The regime of Cuban President **Carlos Prío Socarrás** is ended by an almost bloodless coup d'état headed by former President **Fulgencio Batista** (shown). The deposed president flees to Mexico shortly after two palace guards are slain. Batista says he intends to maintain law and order as a friend of the people until a free election.

Coup in Egypt

Egypt's **King Farouk** abdicates as General **Mohammed Naguib** (shown) takes control in a bloodless coup d'état. Naguib promises a much-needed reform program even as Egypt is placed under martial law after mobs destroy U.S., British and French businesses in Cairo.

1952 Advertisement

Only those inside Convention Hall in Chicago were able to see the nomination of Abraham Lincoln in 1860. Now millions can see the conventions via television.

TODAY YOU GET A CLEARER PICTURE

Don't miss the political conventions in July. See them clearly on **WESTINGHOUSE TELEVISION** with the Electronic Clarifier

You'll get the best picture of this exciting presidential race if you watch the Westinghouse telecasts over CBS-TV on a Westinghouse set. Westinghouse offers a new combination of basic technical advances that produces the most completely reliable television performance you've ever seen. The amazing Electronic Clarifier and exclusive Single Dial Tuning give clear pictures that stay clear without dial fiddling.

PICK THE WINNER! We invite you to compare the performance of the new Westinghouse sets with any other make. Compare prices, too. You'll find you can own a Westinghouse without spending extra money.

HUGE 21" PICTURE. CAMPAIGN SPECIAL Model 2121. An election-year special! Your opportunity to own a top-performing, big-screen Westinghouse at the lowest price ever offered for this quality. Mahogany table model or, with matching legs, no table required. Your Westinghouse dealer offers easy terms, low down payment, big trade-in allowance. See him today!

WESTINGHOUSE TELEVISION WITH THE ELECTRONIC CLARIFIER GIVES YOU CLEAR PICTURES THAT STAY CLEAR. Another first for Westinghouse engineers. Another reason why you can be sure...if it's Westinghouse.

NO STREAKS   NO FLUTTER   NO FLOP-OVER

Tune in on today's Westinghouse presented complete on both the Republican and the CBS-TV and CBS Radio Networks beginning July 6.

YOU CAN BE <u>SURE</u>...IF IT'S Westinghouse

Let The

PRESIDENTIAL GAMES
Begin!

Democratic presidential nominee **Adlai Stevenson** and his running mate, Senator **John Sparkman** of Alabama, meet with President **Harry S. Truman** at the White House for a strategy session.

Republicans **Dwight D. Eisenhower** and **Richard Nixon** are up to the challenge.

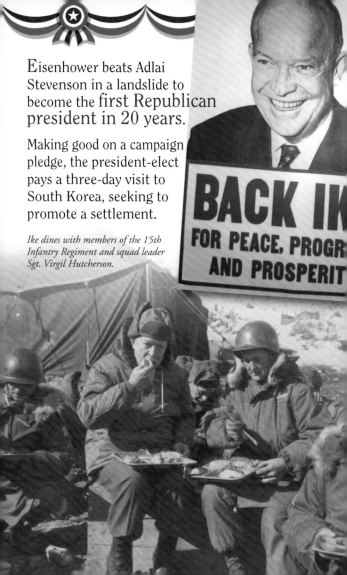

Eisenhower beats Adlai Stevenson in a landslide to become the first Republican president in 20 years.

Making good on a campaign pledge, the president-elect pays a three-day visit to South Korea, seeking to promote a settlement.

Ike dines with members of the 15th Infantry Regiment and squad leader Sgt. Virgil Hutcherson.

BACK IK
FOR PEACE, PROGR
AND PROSPERIT

My name is **Humphrey Bogart**, for those of you in the audience who are either too old or too young to know who I am.

I've been asked by the Treasury Department to tell you about the improved E Bond. In a way I suppose I'm sort of a salesman. Although I personally don't think that E Bonds need selling. You ought to be knocking on Uncle Sam's door to buy 'em. You see, I'm not selling you used cars, television sets, sewing machines, etc., etc. I'm selling you a stake in the future of America and the safety and security of all of us.

This new improved E Bond pays you three percent. If you hold full time, ten years after maturity, you'll get back twice as much money or almost twice as much money as you put in to it. In other words you almost double your dough. Now I think that's a pretty fair proposition.

The United States government stands squarely behind these bonds, now even better."

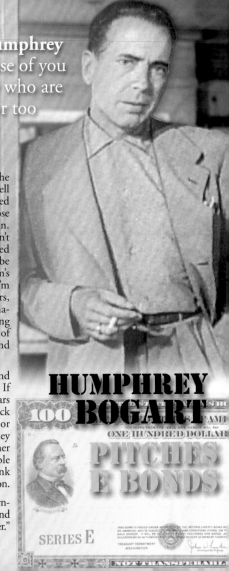

HUMPHREY BOGART
PITCHES E BONDS

150 Extra Engineers

An IBM Electronic Calculator speeds throug thousands of intricate computations so quick that on many complex problems it's just like havin 150 EXTRA Engineers.

No longer must valuable engineering personnel ... now in critical shortage ... spend pricele creative time at routine repetitive figuring.

Thousands of IBM Electronic Business Machin ... vital to our nation's defense ... are at work f science, industry, and the armed forces, in labor tories, factories, and offices, helping to meet urge demands for greater production.

IBM INTERNATIONAL BUSINESS MACHIN

-GI BECOMES BLONDE BEAUTY

Operations Transform Bronx Youth

MDs RULE CHR '100% WOMAN

DAILY NEWS
NEW YORK'S PICTURE NEWSPAPER

ned Woman
me for Yule

A Werd of a

Former U.S. Army clerk, 26-year-old George Jorgensen, Jr., creates a stir after he undergoes a series of operations in Copenhagen to change his sex from male to female. On her return to New York, the glamorous **Christine Jorgensen** tells a phalanx of reporters that she's very happy to be back home and that she doesn't have any definite plans at the moment, and ends by saying: "…I thank you all for coming, but I think it's too much."

Celebrating its 100th anniversary, *Marshal Field's* Chicago store invites some former employees to dinner, including movie director **Vincente Minnelli** (dressed windows), **Burt Lancaster** (floor-walker) **Arlene Dahl** (lingerie model, pictured here), and **Dorothy Lamour** (elevator operator).

Pacific Mills, makers of Catalina Swimwear, founds the *Miss Universe* pageant. **Armi Kuusela** from Finland is declared the winner at the first contest, held in Long Beach, California.

There she is... The new Miss America *is* **Colleen Hutchins** *from Salt Lake City, Utah.*

IT'S A CRIME

Bank robber **Willie "the actor" Sutton** is caught and sentenced to 30 to 120 years in Attica State Prison. Sutton famously once answered a reporter who asked why he robbed banks, "because that's where the money is." Sutton's estimated lifetime take: $2 million.

Arnold Schuster, the amateur detective responsible for Sutton's apprehension, is shot and killed near his Brooklyn home on the orders of Gambino family mob boss **Albert Anastasia**.

The U.S. Court of Appeals in New York unanimously upholds the conviction of underworld czar **FRANK COSTELLO** for contempt of the Senate Crime Committee for walking out of an open hearing last year. Sentenced to 18 months in prison, Costello is driven in his private limousine to the courthouse where he surrenders to U.S. marshals. The U.S. Department of Justice petitions for cancellation of Costello's citizenship.

- FRIENDS IN HIGH PLACES -

A New York crime probe uncovers close personal relationships between Sicilian-born underworld figure **Thomas "3-Finger" Luchese** and leading city, state and federal officials as well as political figures. His U.S. citizenship is cancelled on the grounds he falsified his naturalization papers.

With Justice Hugo L. Black dissenting, the death sentences of convicted atomic spies **ETHEL** and **JULIUS ROSENBERG**, above, are upheld by the U.S. Supreme Court.

THE LONG, LONG ARM OF THE LAW

Ralph "Bottles" Capone, brother of the late infamous Al, is indicted on charges of income tax evasion for failing to settle a tax bill of $92,667 dating back to 1922-1928.

Josephine Baker files a $400,000 defamation suit against columnist Walter Winchell on the grounds he wrote articles attacking her following an incident at New York's posh Stork Club, which refused to serve her.

And in a speech given in Buenos Aires on racial discrimination in America, Baker says "the U.S. is not a free country... I do not envy those who live there."

Singer **Paul Robeson** is barred from singing in the Oakland Municipal Auditorium because of his leftist political views.

ERROL FLYNN breaks his ankle while filming a movie fight at Universal Studios.

✚ Comedienne **Martha Raye** is flown to a Miami Beach hospital after being stricken with a severe intestinal attack while vacationing in Jamaica.

✚ **Glenn Ford** is thrown from his horse during filming and suffers three broken ribs and bruises.

✚ Recovering after an appendectomy, **Marilyn Monroe** is discharged from a Hollywood hospital.

Despite surgeons finding a "Do Not Open Till Christmas" sign on his chest, comedian **RED SKELTON** undergoes surgery for an acute abdominal problem.

Marilyn

Star on the Rise

Monroe

Marilyn Monroe appears in *Monkey Business* where she is seen for the first time as a platinum blonde, and she begins filming *Gentlemen Prefer Blondes*.

Marilyn is Grand Marshall of the Miss America beauty pageant in Atlantic City.

When studio head Darryl Zanuck finds out that Marilyn posed nude for a calendar, he and other studio executives instruct her to deny that she is the girl in the picture, saying that her career will be ruined if she admits the truth. Instead, Marilyn goes before the press and tells the truth and receives an overwhelmingly favorable reaction from the public.

Marilyn seeks legal action against photographer Tom Kelly to stop him from allowing the use of her nude photo on such items as ashtrays and highball glasses.

Marilyn receives more than 5,000 letters a week from admirers with one U.S. battalion in Korea offering to marry her.

MAGAZINES

New for '52

KFC begins franchising in 1952.

No-Cal *is the first diet soda.*

Ban is the first roll-on deodorant.

The first Holiday Inn opens in Memphis, Tennessee.

roll on
ban...
oll out
oubt!

Today's **ban** rolls on the

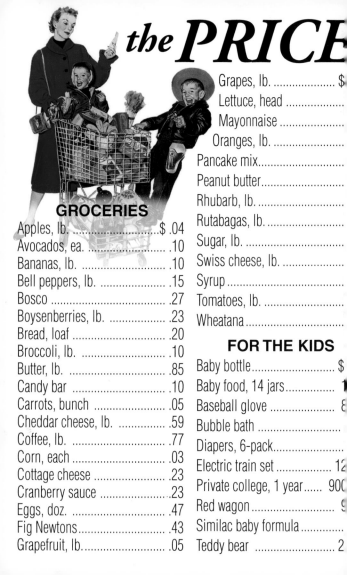

the PRICE

Grapes, lb.	$
Lettuce, head	
Mayonnaise	
Oranges, lb.	
Pancake mix	
Peanut butter	
Rhubarb, lb.	
Rutabagas, lb.	
Sugar, lb.	
Swiss cheese, lb.	
Syrup	
Tomatoes, lb.	
Wheatana	

GROCERIES

Apples, lb.	$ .04
Avocados, ea.	.10
Bananas, lb.	.10
Bell peppers, lb.	.15
Bosco	.27
Boysenberries, lb.	.23
Bread, loaf	.20
Broccoli, lb.	.10
Butter, lb.	.85
Candy bar	.10
Carrots, bunch	.05
Cheddar cheese, lb.	.59
Coffee, lb.	.77
Corn, each	.03
Cottage cheese	.23
Cranberry sauce	.23
Eggs, doz.	.47
Fig Newtons	.43
Grapefruit, lb.	.05

FOR THE KIDS

Baby bottle	$
Baby food, 14 jars	1
Baseball glove	8
Bubble bath	
Diapers, 6-pack	
Electric train set	12
Private college, 1 year	900
Red wagon	9
Similac baby formula	
Teddy bear	2

f THINGS

FOR HIM

...efcase	$ 22.95
...mb	.05
...rcut	1.00
...cktie	2.00
...oes	17.94
...tson hat	10.00
...t	98.00
...derwear	.19

FOR HER

...use	$ 5.95
...hmere sweater	21.95
...enhower jacket	12.95
...ves	2.98
...d cream	.98
...stick	1.00
...vado bracelet watch	270.00
...ticoat	3.98
...oes	8.95-14.95
...cks	17.98
...ckings	1.65
...eta skirt	14.95
...ol suit	65.00

ENTERTAINMENT

...pm record	$ .89
...key game	.70
...el, Miami Beach	14.00
...vie ticket	adult .50, kid .20
...v York City Opera	1.50-3.60

HOUSING

3 br. house, Chappaqua, NY	$ 32,500
3 br. apt., New York City	32,500
3 br. house, Santa Monica, CA	17,300

WEEKLY SALARIES

Accountant	$ 60.00
Bank teller	65.00
Beauty operator	50.00
Cashier	55.00
Copywriter	95.00
Librarian	66.00
Machinist	81.00
Marilyn Monroe	750.00
Nurse	80.00
Photographer	55.00
Salesman	90.00
Secretary	55.00
Truck driver	70.00
Waitress	40.00

STOCKS

Boeing Airplane	$ 47 1/2
Decca Records	8 5/8
Eastman Kodak	45
General Motors	50 3/8
Gulf Oil	52 1/2
Magnavox	16
Rexall Drug	5 3/8
RKO Pictures	3 3/4
Safeway Stores	34
Sears Roebuck	61 3/8

ONLY LIFE BRAS BY FORMFIT ARE

"Triple Fitted" to You

Fashion '52

Givenchy presents his first couture collection. **Dior** shows black dresses and evening dresses with wide skirts.

Elsa Schiaparelli complains that designers have forgotten to make clothes that fit well with womanly attributes such as breasts and hips, and have instead focused on thin, model-type figures.

The shirtwaist dress has a form-fitting bodice and a wide skirt, and is available in various patterns and colors.

Suits are more loosely constructed than previous seasons. Spencer jackets over full skirts are a definite hit.

Waists are cinched with figure-flattering belts and built-in waistbands, adding texture and drama to day and evening wear.

A wonderful way

to spend your day!

Relax in Ship'n Shore's

newest combed gingham

sport blouse

Stained glass colors,

ever lovely...

ever washable.

Sizes 30 to 40.

3.50

Ship'n Shore®

BLOUSES

1952
swimwear

UNMISTAKABLY ASCOT

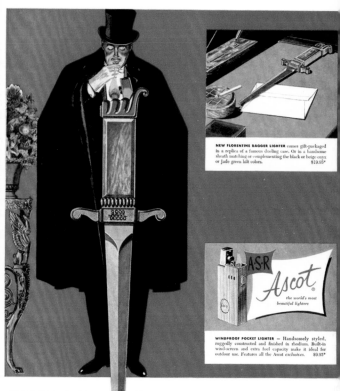

NEW FLORENTINE DAGGER LIGHTER comes gift-packaged in a replica of a famous dueling case. Or in a handsome sheath matching or complementing the black or beige onyx or Jade green hilt colors. $19.95*

the world's most beautiful lighters

WINDPROOF POCKET LIGHTER — Handsomely styled, ruggedly constructed and finished in rhodium. Built-in wind-screen and extra fuel capacity make it ideal for outdoor use. Features all the Ascot exclusives. $9.95*

MORE INTENSE SPARKS WITH ASCOT FLINTS

Made to Ascot's special formula, Ascot Flints produce more intense, quicker-firing sparks in any lighter. Next time, ask for Ascot Flints!

Most dramatic lighter of the year — the Florentine Dagger by Ascot. Lighter . . . letter o . . . paperweight and distinguished desk ornament all in one, the Florentine's distin Renaissance design and authentic detail make it a lighter to be prized, a gift to be treas At smarter stores, coast-to-coast. • *Mfrs. Tax Incl. Other models from $6.95 to $250.00*

SPORTS

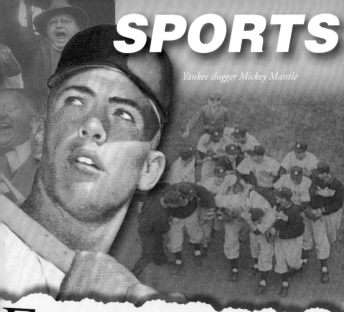

Yankee slugger Mickey Mantle

Fans go wild as the New York Yankees beat the Brooklyn Dodgers four games to three to win their 4th straight World Championship.

Most Valuable Player

National League
Hank Sauer (Chicago)

American League
Bobby Shantz (Philadelphia)

Strikeouts

National League
Warren Spahn (Boston, 183)

American League
Allie Reynolds (New York, 160)

Batting Champions

National League
Stan Musial (St. Louis, .336)

American League
Ferris Fain (Philadelphia, .327)

Home Run Leaders

National League
Ralph Kiner (Pittsburgh, 37)
Hank Sauer (Chicago, 37)

American League
Larry Doby (Cleveland, 32)

Stan Musial

FOOTBALL

NATIONAL FOOTBALL LEAGUE CHAMPIONS

Detroit Lions over Cleveland Browns, 17-7

ROSE BOWL

Illinois over Stanford, 40-7

HEISMAN TROPHY

Billy Vessels, Oklahoma, HB

NATIONAL COLLEGE FOOTBALL CHAMPIONS

Michigan State

Detroit Lions quarter-back Bobby Layne

BOBBIE 'BLONDE BOMBER' LAYNE

BASKETBALL

NBA CHAMPIONS

Minneapolis Lakers over New York Knicks, 4-3

NBA SEASON SCORING LEADER

Paul Arizin, Philadelphia 1,674 points (25.4 avg.)

NBA ALL-STAR GAME

East over West, 108-91

NCAA CHAMPIONS

Kansas over St. John's, 80-63

Lakers' George Mikan

ROCKY **MARCIANO** **DEFEATS** "JERSEY" JOE **WALCOTT**

Marciano

Marciano is knocked down in the first round by the aging **Walcott**.

Marciano comes back strong in the 13th with a right-hand jaw crusher which KO's **Walcott**.

It is Rocky's 43rd consecutive victory, making him the first unbeaten heavyweight to win the title as well. The year's most dramatic battle is seen coast-to-coast via closed-circuit TV in 31 cities.

HEAVYWEIGHT

"Jersey" Joe Walcott

Rocky Marciano

LIGHT HEAVYWEIGHT

Joey Maxim

Archie Moore

MIDDLEWEIGHT

Sugar Ray Robinson

WELTERWEIGHT

Kid Gavilan

LIGHTWEIGHT

James Carter

Lauro Salas

FEATHERWEIGHT

Sandy Saddler

1952 Advertisement

Kodak

For color pictures at their finest...

Kodak's newest "miniature"... with coupled range-finder

Has superb Kodak Ektar $f/3.5$ lens ...
unsurpassed for sharp, brilliant color slides
for projection or full-color prints. Also
coupled range-finder, automatic controls,
1/300 flash shutter. This superlative
camera is agreeably priced at $92.50,
including Federal Tax. Flasholder, $8.25.
At your Kodak dealer's ...
Eastman Kodak Company, Rochester 4, N. Y.

Prices are subject to change without notice

Kodak Signet 35 Camera

70,000 Attend the Opening of the 15th Summer Olympic Games at Helsinki.

1952
XV OLYMPIA
HELSINKI

The big story of the Olympics is the participation of Soviet teams. Along with a temporary smile of good fellowship, they bring their own scoring system. "We won," they tell the home folks.

Everyone else is busy applauding Czechoslovakian Emil Zátopek, who breaks the exisiting Olympic record in 3 track events.

After 16 days of competition, Uncle Sam's star-spangled athletes achieve their greatest Olympic triumph ever at Helsinki, winning 40 gold medals and 76 medals total—more than any other nation.

For fun-filled trips to
Winter Playgrounds...

See this Man— he'll help you plan 'em

YOUR GREYHOUND AGENT

THIS YEAR, take all or part of your vacation in Winter—when you need it most!

We know a man who can show you how to relax in Southern sun at scarcely more cost than staying home! He's the Greyhound agent in your town—and he'll arrange your trip in easy-riding, well-warmed coaches, select optional scenic routes and stopovers... he can even make hotel reservations and plan special sightseeing. All this at rates so far below those of conventional travel that you can spend extra days in the sun.

Your Greyhound agent (man or woman) will explain the advantages of *Limited* schedules, with extra luxury—or *Express* service, which will take you straight through at no extra fare, often without change of bus or baggage.

Start planning *now*—and see your Greyhound agent soon—he'll make your plans come true!

Florida and Gulf Coast—Luxury Limited schedules to the sunny South. Vacation begins when you board a Super-Coach!

California, Pacific Coast—Time-saving Express service to all the West. Go straight through or enjoy scenic stopovers

All the Southwest—It's the top of the season in the sunny Southwest! There are no lower fares than Greyhound's.

Snow Sports Everywhere—well-warmed coaches to winter wonderlands. Charter a Greyhound for you

GREYHOUND

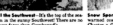

Today's Best Buy in Travel

SEND FOR FREE PICTORIAL TRAVEL BOOK

Mail to GREYHOUND INFORMATION CENTER, 105 W. MADISON, CHICAGO, ILL. for free 16-page pictorial booklet describing pre-planned all-America!

NAME_____

ADDRESS_____

CITY_____STATE_____

Born in 1952

Dan Aykroyd	Robin Quivers
Clive Barker	Christopher Reeve
Roseanne Barr	Paul Reubens
David Byrne	Herb Ritts
Jimmy Connors	Isabella Rossellini
Stewart Copeland	Gus Van Sant
Bob Costas	Randy Savage
Maureen Dowd	Vikram Seth
Jeff Goldblum	George Strait
John Goodman	Joe Strummer
Marilu Henner	Patrick Swayze
John Lone	Mr. T
Walter Mosley	Amy Tan
Liam Neeson	Julie Taymor
Laraine Newman	Bill Walton
Sharon Osbourne	Robert Zemeckis

Dan Aykroyd

Maureen Dowd

Joe Strummer

Walter Mosley

Isabella Rossellini

DIED IN **1952**

Paul Éluard
poet

John Garfield
actor

Knut Hamsun
writer

Fletcher Henderson
musician

Curly Howard
comedian

Gertrude Lawrence
actress

Hattie McDaniel
actress

Maria Montessori
educator

Eva Perón
Argentine First Lady

George Santayana
writer

Chaim Weizmann
President of Israel

Paramahansa Yogananda
guru

John Garfield